Find Your Writing Voice

FIND YOUR WRITING VOICE

Chris Brogan

Owner Media Group, Inc
Boston

This book was produced using Pressbooks.com, and PDF rendering was done by PrinceXML.

DEDICATION

To my eventual mother-in-law Joan. You are vibrant and full of life and always in the middle of living out interesting stories. To your voice being ever present.

CONTENTS

TABLE OF CONTENTS

Christopher E Brogan

INTRODUCTION

Introduction – Your Voice is You

If you and I were sitting down for coffee (or tea or beer or smoothies), I'd probably ask you a question like "Tell me something that gets you excited these days." You'd take a breath, look up (people always do, as if their memories are literally in the air over their heads), maybe smile a little, and you'd tell me something.

More than likely, you'd start with a word like "well" or "Hmm, let's see," but then you'd decide what to tell me.

"I'm really into food, so I started a blog about food. Only, I'm not a chef, and I'm not any kind of an expert or anything. I just love food. I like stories about it. I watch lots of cooking shows. I'm just REALLY into food!"

I might ask, "Oh, do you cook?"

"Not really," and you'd laugh. "I can follow a recipe, if forced. But you'd be appalled. I microwave a lot of stuff. But no, I don't cook a lot."

"You see, I'm an athlete, a bodybuilding competitor – they call it a figure competitor – and so I'm often on a pretty strict diet. This has the added side effect of making me think about food a lot. Like, obsess!"

I'd laugh. Your eyes would wrinkle a bit.

"Yeah, and I have a few weird preferences too. My fiance (and lots of other people) can't believe I prefer my steak well done. Like burned done. Like dead. And I sometimes put ketchup in my tuna fish."

I'd agree that you're weird. We'd laugh. And then maybe I'd ask about your blog.

"Well, it's tricky. I'm having trouble writing the articles the way I want, because I know what I want to say but I just can't get it to come out right. Sometimes, I over explain. Other times, I get caught up in some little detail. Half the time, I just feel like a fraud because I'm not qualified to talk about cooking and food."

Writing and Communicating Can Really Gnarl Us Up

If you ever wanted to pretend to be a research scientist, I could give you a fun project.

- Use your phone to record video.
- Ask someone to talk about what they're really passionate about.
- Then ask them to write it into a small essay.

What you'll see is amazing. Talking only in body language, you'll see a bright smile, sparkling eyes, expansive hand gesture when they talk about what they're into. The moment you open a laptop and ask them to write about it, you'll see hunched shoulders, a frown, lots of face rubbing.

Somehow, that "last mile" between what we know and then expressing how we want to talk about it is REALLY HARD for a lot of people.

For others, it's not that it's difficult, but it ends up feeling like no one is reading what you're writing or that no one cares.

I'm here to help in both cases. If you want to write better, find your voice, and learn how to write in a way that's the best of what you're thinking and talking about, I know that I can help you get there.

This book is written with action in mind. It's not about theory. We have to get you in the game and keep you there. No one learns much just by reading and thinking about it. We have to DO SOMETHING. You with me?

A Little Bit About Me

I'm Chris Brogan. I'm the New York Times bestselling author of eight books (this one's my ninth), with plenty more to come. I started blogging in 1998 (they used to call it journaling), and my words and ideas have led me to work with the biggest companies in the world (folks like Sony, Disney, Google, Coke) and to be on TV with Dr Phil and to interview people like Sir Richard Branson.

Heck, I even got to meet a princess, all because she knew my writing.

I'm not the best writer. I'm not the smartest. I'm not the most successful. But I'm a great writer, reasonably smart, and successful enough that my little fingers pay the bills and run a media and education company.

When I'm not writing, I'm into fitness, video games (XBOXOne, baby!), nerdy stuff, and family. I'm engaged to Jacqueline Carly, and between us, we have three kids. I like 90s hip hop, heavy metal, and whatever you call those soulful rock bands like the Black Keys, the White Stripes and the Alabama Shakes.

That's me.

The Rest of the Book

You've seen the Table of Contents. I started there, by the way. I wrote the title of the book, wrote the table of contents, and then sent it to Jacq to see if it was the kind of book she'd want to read. She said yes, so I started writing it.

Here's what we'll cover:

Chapter 01 – Our Destination: A Great Writing Voice – If you don't start with the goal in mind, how will you know you've reached it?

Chapter 02 – The Kitchen Table Laboratory of Writ-

ing – Part of what locks you up is that you take writing too seriously, and treat it like it's fragile. I'll fix that!

Chapter 03 – Use A Simple Writing Frame – This is one of the keys to my success. I'll give it to you. Here, have a key!

Chapter 04 – Make Those Words Match The Real You – Writing is this weird thing where we start talking funny, nothing like how we'd tell a friend. I'll help with that.

Chapter 05 – How to Find Topics to Write About – Maybe you're stuck in the ideas department. I've got a few good ideas that can get you there.

Chapter 06 – Project Thinking – How to Get More Done – I know, I know. Writing takes time and it feels challenging to find that. I can help, and I can get you from weird ideas to published work, even if that "published" is that email you've been meaning to send your brother.

Chapter 07 – The World is Waiting to Hear From You – Take action and get your work out there. We need to hear from you, and someone out there is really going to love what you have to say.

That's the Book

That's what you've got in store for you, pally wally! Let's dig right in and start developing that writing voice of yours.

Oh! One Last Thing!

This book doesn't have a ton of pages because it's meant for you to actually DO SOMETHING and take action. I'll tell you a secret or two that I know from having been involved in books since 2008.

1. People do judge books by their covers.
2. People judge books by their page count.
3. People judge books by their price.

Know what? None of those things actually matter, per se. A book is valuable if YOU find something in it that will change your life in some meaningful way. Why would I ever use more words and fill up more pages when the goal is making you successful?

Wherever I can, I'll share more "secrets" like this with you. If I can demystify some of the things people think about books and publishing and the writer's life, I'll gladly do that.

Let's get this thing going, okay?

(One final note: my favorite book editor I ever worked with told me that I have some weird affinity for the word "thing." She removed over a thousand instances of that word in a reasonably small book I wrote for her company. She's not editing this book, so beware. It's part of my "voice.")

1

CHAPTER 01 - OUR DESTINATION: A GREAT WRITING VOICE

Chris Brogan

Chapter 01 – Our Destination: A Great Writing Voice

What the heck is a "writing voice," anyway? I imagine that you have a sense of this or you wouldn't have bought this book. I mean, it'd be a weird impulse buy otherwise. But just in case, I'll start there.

Literature people use the word "voice" to mean something more like the style in which a book is written. For you and me, we'll define "writing voice" to mean the act of taking the best version of you and how you communicate and translating that to the written word.

A little further down, I'll give you six specific attributes you can use as gauges and begin working on the details of your writing voice. For now, here's a quick definition.

Writing voice = your best self captured in words.

Good? Good!

If you are one of the 3% of people who read introductions (I'm definitely one of them, and you should go back there, dang it!), you'll already know that MY voice is very conversational and very personable. I write as if you and I are sitting across from each other having a cup of coffee (or whatever it is you drink).

That's my voice. It might be yours, too. But if you've ever met me in person or if you ever meet me, you'll think, "Oh wow. I feel like I already know you because you talk just like you write."

That's the point.

Obviously, this isn't 100% accurate. Right? Because when we talk, we stutter a bit, we mumble, we maybe have a bunch of verbal tics, like adding "you know?" to the end of everything we say. I've got friends who use the F word in place of spaces (a sentence would look like : thatFNguyFNcutFNmeFNoffFNFer!!)

Our goal is to get you writing better, writing faster (because once you get the hang of this, you'll write faster), and writing more about what you want to cover.

I start all projects with a goal. If you're not aiming at something, how will you know that you've succeeded? Since you're along for the ride, you've got to make some goals with me right now. Let's go.

Commit to a Goal With Me

Here it is: "I promise to complete 100% of the exercises Chris gives me throughout this book."

That's your goal: 100% of all writing exercises complete.

Send me a quick note and it'll take only 3 minutes tops.

So That Was Weird

I'm pretty sure you've never read a book where the author asked you to commit to something within the first few pages. Did you actually do it? If you didn't, it tells me a few details about you:

- You're cautious
- You worry that it's a gimmick (It's a trap!)
- You're rushing through this

I'm also doing this to show you another way that you

can find your writing voice. You can encourage interaction, if that's part of who you are. Writing doesn't have to be a one way street, is what I'm saying.

Also, I really love feedback and interaction so starting with that commitment helps.

Finally, I'll be putting writing exercises all throughout the book. No better way for us to learn than to practice. So, that's that about our commitment for now.

Goals and Destinations

One way to make your writing better almost immediately is to write with your destination in mind. You probably think of the word "goal" as something big or something lofty. That's why I also used the word "destination," but you pick whichever resonates with you. Let's dig in.

Think about the difference between chatting with someone versus approaching them to talk about something specific. In a chat, there's no real structure. You mostly focus on the back and forth. If you've got to tell a friend that you think what they said to the receptionist the other day was rude, you're going to probably work on how you're going to say it.

When I write a blog post, I always have two simultaneous goals:

- Help my reader with something in their lives
- Encourage my reader to do more business with me (or at least stay connected to me)

Beyond this, every post I write has a set goal. For instance, if I decide I'm going to write about how to set up a simple website, here's how my thought process works:

- The post is about setting up a website
- First paragraph should ensure readers that they're in the right place and that they're smart enough
- Next paragraph should start the step-by-step instructions
- Finish with action steps the reader can take
- Okay, now review and ensure it serves the reader AND me (mostly the reader)
- Publish

Something like that goes through my mind. This covers the GOAL or destination part of the writing. And that helps with your voice in this way:

- If you have a sense of where you're going with your writing, you'll be able to think more about how you want to get there.
- The actual writing is the goal. How you get there is the voice. Make sense?

Now you know that having a goal or target or destination is one important part of developing your voice. It's not the MOST important part, but it's something you can work on right away.

Destinations are Contextual

The point of finding a destination/goal is to put it in context of what your writing project is. So if you have a blog about leadership, than every post you're going to write should in some way lead people to a lesson or advice or action around leadership.

If the purpose of your writing is to entertain people with material you find interesting, you need merely entertain them. Maybe your destinations all have some kind of twist in mind.

Also, maybe you write just for yourself. It still counts as writing. I'll tell you my personal bias. To me, if you're not hoping to put your work in the hands of others, you're missing the heart of writing. Others may disagree.

Another way to say this is to think about genre. If you watch a murder mystery, you know someone will die at the beginning, and that the point of the story is to solve the crime. If you watch a documentary, you know every-thing in it is built to be true.

Destinations and goals in your writing are about mak-ing sure that you stick to a frame's expectations.

Another Example of a Goal/Destination:

If you were going to write a memoir, the goal is to share your life experiences such that people might com-pare/contrast their own lives with yours. There are many great essayists who do this, some with comedy and others with sadness. David Sedaris is great for realism. Mary Karr for a more somber read.

- First paragraph would start us right in the action
- Second paragraph might explain your world a bit
- Third paragraph gets into more details
- Fourth probably same as the third
- Last paragraph reflects on the experience and/ or offers any potential insight
- Call to action might be inviting people to compare/contrast their experience

Let's lock this into practice:

ACTION: Start Every Piece of Writing with a Goal/ Destination

This is a simple action for you to practice. Every time you plan to write anything (blog post, newsletter, email, your amazing novel), start by stating (even just in your head) the goal of the piece.

That's it. That's your action for the goals/destination part. I'm asking you to do it. Promise?

—

Elements of a Great Writing Voice

What goes into your writing voice is the clever use of the following ingredients:

- Tone – how casual or formal or colloquial your writing is
- Word choice – how you phrase what you write
- Sentence length – how long or short your sentences are
- Comprehension – how easy it is to understand your ideas
- Imagery – how well you paint pictures with your words
- Storytelling – can you get people from one part of your writing to the goal?

Let's look at each of these, and then we can start practicing on a few sample projects after. Okay?

Tone – I write in a very casual tone. This is on purpose as I want you to feel more like we're talking over coffee more than I want you to think of me as some kind of teacher at a lectern. The tone of what you write is important. All the attributes contribute to how people think about your voice, but this one and maybe Imagery are what people remember about how they feel about you based on your writing.

Word Choice – I can tell you that word choice is kind of a secret weapon of mine. I use small words more often than not. I also like unique words and phrases, because people hate to read cliches. Which words you use really matters to your projects, but not in any kind of "you've gotta be smart about it" way. Instead, the idea is that you can really drive towards what sets your writing apart here. (My fiance Jacq likes using made up words like "bestest" in her work. I do, too!)

Sentence Length – I love small sentences. Big sentences can be scary. However, if you only write small or big sentences, your reader will get lulled into a rhythm and will likely come to regret it, even if they don't immediately notice it's happening. Shorter sentences rule. But mix it up, okay?

Comprehension – Can people understand what you're trying to tell them? Sometimes, we get complex in our word choice or we over-explain something, or worse, we presume everyone knows what we're talking about and we under explain it. This one takes a lot of practice. But it's an attribute of your voice. Do people "get" what you're trying to tell them? (Might require another set of eyes to practice and improve.)

Imagery – Last night, I made my kids hot dogs. I split open fresh, yeasty-smelling buns and slathered on ketchup on one, ketchup and mustard on the next, and mustard and tart dill relish on mine. The hot dogs were near bursting with juicy flavor, and they tasted like summer baseball games played on a fresh cut lawn with a cold lemonade in hand. Imagery is like that. Can you paint scenes into your reader's minds?

Storytelling – My imagery example above is also a storytelling example. Story is the most effective teacher humans have. We use story as a mental blueprint before practicing anything, before researching, etc. Connect people to a story around what you're writing, and you'll deliver lots more value.

Don't Feel Too Daunted By All This

If you read through those attributes and start to get a queasy feeling, please don't. It's all good. You're already doing all this. You're just not as conscious of it and you're not likely at the levels you want to be with regards to some parts of it.

I repeat: you're already writing with some kind of tone, word choice, sentence length, etc etc etc.

Our job together, though, is to get you to write BETTER and to find that writing voice. That's the whole purpose of this book. You're here because you want to take what you have and get it closer to what you WANT to have.

We've got two more actions and then we'll dig into the second chapter.

Action: Rate yourself on your CURRENT level of ability

There's no judgment in knowing where you stand. Think about you in a car turning on your GPS. The computer needs to know three details:

1. Where you are
2. Where you're going

3. The best route to take

With that in mind, I want you to rate yourself on a scale of 1-10 as to how you feel about your own abilities in the six attributes of voice

- Tone – how casual or formal or colloquial your writing is
- Word choice – how you phrase what you write
- Sentence length – how long or short your sentences are
- Comprehension – how easy it is to understand your ideas
- Imagery – how well you paint pictures with your words
- Storytelling – can you get people from one part of your writing to the goal?

Swing by THIS PAGE and rate yourself where you stand right now. We'll do this a few times throughout the book.

Action: Writing Practice (20 Minutes)

Here's a writing practice assignment. Don't skip these. I promise they'll help a lot in the process.

- Set a timer for 20 minutes. (You can use this if you want. I have one of these.)
- The topic is "My favorite meal."

- Write for 20 minutes on this topic. In it, remember what we've covered above:
  - Goal/destination
  - Tone
  - Word choice
  - Sentence length
  - Comprehension
  - Imagery
  - Storytelling
- Avoid cliches
- Don't worry about how good it is. Just do the writing for now
- Don't let yourself get stuck. Just keep moving forward

When you're done, feel free to share it with our little online group. This is private and you'll be among friends. No one will be there to criticize you, as they're in the same boat. They, like you, want to write better.

Good?

Coming Up Next

From here, where we've set our destination and also looked at the starting points of what we're going to work on through this book, let's head over to the next chapter.

Chapter 02 – The Kitchen Table Laboratory of Writing

In the next chapter, we'll work on everything from writing setups (how and where to get your writing going) to tools (some software, some paper) to everything else we can get into to help that writing voice come out of you like a perfect song. Okay?

Woo!

(Who ends a chapter with "woo?" Me!)

—

2

CHAPTER 02 - THE KITCHEN TABLE LABORATORY OF WRITING

Chris Brogan

Chapter 02 – The Kitchen Table Laboratory of Writing

Imagine sitting down at your desk in your favorite chair with your laptop or a pen and a pad of paper. When I say "pad of paper," I mean something easy going like one of those yellow legal pads, not something fancy like a Moleskine journal. Maybe there's some music playing in the background. Maybe not. (I write in silence. Others can't really stand it to be too quiet). You've got a drink beside you. It's a great writing environment.

I have to tell you something that's true of all successful writers: they are almost all quite accomplished at being able to write pretty much anywhere using any tool. What they least worry about is having everything "perfect" before they sit down to write. That's kind of a myth: that you need the most perfect writing environment.

That's one reason why I called this chapter the Kitchen Table Laboratory of Writing. There's something perfect about the kitchen table as an analogy for easygoing and part of the fabric of everyday life. Some people's kitchen tables are messy. You might have a stack of magazines in one corner of it. Maybe there's a kid nearby doing homework. Or a spouse watching Netflix on his or her tablet.

The other part of it, the laboratory, is about the joy of experimentation, about tools, figuring things out, etc. If writing isn't all that fun, we won't do it all that much, will we? So a kitchen table and a lab. Got it?

I'm writing these words to you at a table that my son usually uses. He's over on his bed. I'm writing the words into a Samsung Galaxy Tab E (about 9 inches across), using an Apple Bluetooth keyboard. I'm writing into Google Docs (all but one of my books was written using Google Docs – Julien Smith made me use Scrivener for The Impact Equation and I didn't like it much).

I wrote Chapter 1 on my laptop, mostly from my bed. I wasn't sick. I just felt like a change of view. Chapter 3 might be written in a hotel room, or partly from my car while waiting for my daughter to come back out of the store.

It's super important to build your writing practice and the tools that support it around the idea that you have to be able to write under a wide variety of circumstances and situations.

To that end, that's what we'll cover in this chapter. We'll talk about practices, habits, and tools to support your writing and the development of your writing voice. Because it all kind of blends together, I'll probably mention everything twice: once in context and once as a kind of resource list near the end of the chapter.

Kitchen Table Writing

Let's break down writing into a few components:

- The idea
- The goal
- The frame
- The writing
- Publishing

Everything from a thought out email to a novel has at least these five core components in the mix. From here on out, I want you to get in the habit of building your writing starting with this.

Take Note: Either with Evernote or a trusted paper

note pad, write down those five bullets above. Use these to start every writing project bigger than a random text message. (We'll add more to the "Take Note" information, so you might put it in an Evernote notebook called "Find Your Writing Voice" or FYWV.)

The Idea – What idea are you putting across? This can sometimes be in its roughest form. Maybe you're thinking about how to write about all the weird food websites you've discovered in your research. The idea might be as simple as "Weird Food Websites I've Found."

The Goal – Your writing must have a goal. Do you want to persuade someone of something? Do you want to inform them? Are you hoping to earn business based on what you wrote? Every piece of writing has to have a goal. The "Weird Food Websites" idea's goal might just be "to entertain people."

The Frame – There are many different ways to write the actual piece. The term frame in this case means the skeleton you write your piece into. What goes into the title, the first paragraph, etc. Things like the Table of Contents involve itself with frames. I'll cover this a bunch more in another chapter.

The Writing – In this case, I mean the actual nitty gritty of sitting down and writing it, but also, I mean your choices and your craft in how you work. Every time you write, be conscious of your effort, of your goals, and of wanting to do the best you can to convey the importance of what you're writing about to the people you hope give you their time to read it.

Publishing – A weird side effect of lacking confidence in your writing is that you tend not to actually publish your work. With regards to doing what you're doing, if you want to find your voice, you have to work through your fear that your writing isn't good enough and you've got to get it out there. (It's the only way to grow.)

With this as the backdrop, the idea of "kitchen table writing" and the "kitchen table laboratory" is that we're working on our writing. It's always a work in progress. It doesn't have to be perfect.

PERMISSION SLIP: your writing doesn't have to be perfect. (Use this whenever you'd like.)

Your voice will come to you the more you practice. I write at least 2000 words a day. You might set yourself the starting goal of 300 Words a Day. Those words I write go into blog posts, newsletters, website copy updates, and books like this one. I never count "practice" words towards my word count. Only productive words. (In fact, I never intentionally practice. I just write on projects.)

One Way to Make Writing Feel Less Intimidating

My friend, James Altucher has method he uses to make writing feel like it's no big deal. He opens up Gmail and starts an email to someone. The "someone" might end up being a chapter in a book or it might be a blog post.

But because it's Gmail and not a blank word document of some kind, it feels less intimidating. When he's done writing, James transfers it over to wherever the final product will reside, be that a blog post, a newsletter article, or a book chapter.

It's definitely one method.

For me, because I've been writing so long, I don't have a whole lot of intimidation with opening up a blank document. But then again, I have a few tricks of my own.

Tricks to Making Writing Less Intimidating

First and foremost, one area where most newer writers have a problem is that they worry about having ideas. The way I deal with that is I keep a folder in Evernote called Ideas. I jot ten ideas a day every day in there. (Stole this from James Altucher's Choose Yourself book.) That way, I'm never at a loss for ideas.

Here are some more tips and tricks, in no particular order:

- Feel free to use a voice recording app to say what's on your mind first, play it back and take notes from that. If you're at work, jot your "in your head" conversation into a text file.

- Put something on the page right away, even if it's junk.
- Leave something for next time, if you're writing a longer piece. Meaning, leave a sentence unfinished so that you know where to pick up when you get back to it.

- Remember that you're writing for one person and that person really wants to hear what you have to say.
- If you write with a laptop or tablet, use software that lets you write offline and online and from multiple computers. For instance:
  - Evernote
  - Google Docs (offline mode with Chrome browser)
  - Microsoft Office 365
- Practice writing everywhere you can, at any time of day, loud or quiet. Get into the habit of producing in any circumstance.

There. Those are a few ideas to help you take the edge off your writing. Let's throw those into a quick practice, okay?

Action: Open up a file (or a blank page) and write 300 words on the topic of "My Childhood Home." Write whatever comes to mind. If you feel like it, share with the group.

Experimenting in the Lab to Find Your Voice

I know earlier in the chapter, I mentioned that we have to publish, and I've also said that practice for practice sake isn't usually all that helpful. I'm about to contradict that for a minute.

You can learn a lot from experimentation. It can even help you improve your writing voice. Remember in the last chapter that I mentioned that "word choice" is part of developing your voice. The bigger picture version of word choice is perspective/point of view.

The exercise above, "My Childhood Home" – how did you approach it? Did you write straightforward and literally about your childhood home? What did you talk about? Did you mention food? Did you talk about people? Did you describe the home itself?

There are so many ways to approach it. Here are five I just came up with on the fly, all about "My Childhood Home:"

- Tell it from my dog's perspective
- Talk about the politics of 1970s America
- Discuss only the appliances
- Imagine what my parents were going through and tell it from that perspective
- Write it from the point of view of real estate and how the average home size is almost double what it was when you were a kid

See? There are lots of ways to experiment with perspective. Further, once you start thinking this way, you can look at the world in other ways. It will start to give you a better point of view from which to write.

I have a friend who runs a site for military special operators. Every post is from a fairly conservative viewpoint, and often with considerations for US and world safety. Every post is written with a serious tone, or with the gallows humor of those types of warriors.

When learning about your voice, you'll start to see even more story ideas, more topics, more ways to think about writing once you have a better and stronger sense of your perspective. If you're a food writer, you'll see every city, state, person, and situation with food in mind.

Action: Write another 300 word post about "The Neighborhood I Remember Most." This time, pick a unique perspective. It's up to you, but if you're stuck, write it as if you were angry about that neighborhood. Or if you were the happiest person there. Or whatever suits your fancy. Feel free to share with the group.

The Tools of the Trade

I warned you that I might have to talk a bit about the tools you can use to write. If you're a pen and paper kind of person, skip this little section. If you're a little more digital, here's a section for you.

- Notes: Evernote – This is a powerful tool for note taking. You can use it in an offline mode, but can also sync it so that you can get your notes on your phone, tablet, laptop, or any Web browser. I can't recommend this enough for a great way to keep your Ideas file for what to write about.

- Writing: Google Docs – This is what I used to write 8 out of my 9 books. If you use the

Chrome web browser, you can write offline or online with Google Docs.

- Writing: Office 365 – Microsoft Word is still a lot of people's favorite.

- Writing: Scrivener – Highly popular with lots of people. A great way to organize larger works. (For Mac only)

- Writing: Ulysses – An alternative to Scrivner. (For Mac only)

- Writing: Here's a list of Windows alternatives to Scrivener and Ulysses.

- Storage: Dropbox – If you want a way to access files from pretty much everywhere.

- Blogging: WordPress – The world's most famous website host.

- Email: MailChimp – A great newsletter platform. See also TinyLetter.

Invariably when I write a list like this, you might say, "Well what about X?" Or "Have you tried Y?" Use whatever you'd like. I have a very successful idea in my life called "The Pirate Ship Approach." It doesn't matter which ship you use, as long as it takes you to the gold.

Put These Tools And Ideas To Use

It's your kitchen table lab, even if your "kitchen table" is the spare room, or the garage, or the tiny shed you built outside your place, or in front of the TV while your kid watches Spongebob. The ideas are simple: experiment, work on your voice, and that work comes from writing and expressing yourself.

Action: Schedule time to write every day. It doesn't have to be the same time every day. But assign yourself a minimum word count of 300 words a day, starting today.

Let's move to the next chapter now. It's a shorter one, with a simple but important concept to teach you. I promise this will improve your writing a lot.

—

3

CHAPTER 03 - USE A SIMPLE WRITING FRAME

Chris Brogan

Chapter 03 – Use A Simple Writing Frame

I briefly mentioned this in the last chapter. Let's get into it. The idea is simple, but not easy. Important, though. That's for sure.

What is a writing frame?

It means a kind of structure. You've heard that stories have a beginning, middle and end. That's a very high level frame. I read Shawn Coyne's amazing book Story Grid which teaches you a LOT about a much more complex writing frame. What I'll share with you is something in the middle.

A frame is a way to think about organizing your words and ideas, so that you can spend more time writing and spend less time worrying how to put something together.

In this chapter, I'll give you a few examples, and you can use them as your frame. I've used the same two frames for pretty much every project I've ever taken on in the last seven or eight years.

What you might also consider, however, is crafting your own frame after you see what goes into it. It's not as hard as it might sound. I promise. Nothing I do is all that difficult.

My Blogging Frame

I've shared this in lots of different ways over the years. Thousands of people have learned and adopted my blogging frame. Yet, when the average person reads their work, they don't say, "Hey, you sound a lot like that Chris Brogan weirdo."

I want to start here because it's an easy one to explain. I use it daily. I use it to write blog posts, newsletter articles, and most everything but books. (I'll share my book frame after.)

- Start with a Catchy Title

- Find a Picture to Accompany the Piece
- First Paragraph – Personable
- Subheading 1 – Echo the Title
- Second Paragraph – Give the main point (the most important info)
- Third Paragraph – Explain, give examples, provide actionable idea
- Fourth (and Fifth if needed) Paragraph- Give More Examples
- Last Paragraph – End with a call to action of some kind

That's it. That's my frame. You can go read most every post I've written at chrisbrogan.com and see it in action.

As you can see, a "frame" isn't all that complicated, but this also gives you as a writer something to work from. You can work on getting your ideas onto the page instead of worry about how to organize the information. I'll give you a pretend post filled out:

- Start with a Catchy Title — Batman Would Make a Great President
- Find a Picture to Accompany the Piece – Picture of Batman (maybe Lego Batman)
- First Paragraph – Personable – I've been a fan of Batman since I was five. It's because he's a normal guy like us. Well, if we were billionaires with murdered parents. …etc
- Subheading 1 – Echo the Title — Batman Would Make a Great President
- Second Paragraph – Give the main point (the

most important info) – He's about self-reliance, but also sticking up for people who need a little help. ... etc.
- Third Paragraph – Explain, give examples, provide actionable idea
- Fourth (and Fifth if needed) Paragraph- Give More Examples
- Last Paragraph – Call to Action – I'd love to hear which fictional character YOU think would make a great president. Share with me here!

See? Easy peasy. You get a taste. By the way, that took about three minutes to write. To actually write around 300-500 words? No more than 20. Partly because I type fast. Partly because I know the subject matter. Mostly because I have that frame in place.

The Elements of a Simple Writing Frame

What goes into a writing frame? It's a tool for organizing information into a useful pattern. That's all you have to think about. What's the best way to organize information such that my reader (and I) will benefit from it?

1. You have to draw people in at the start.
2. You have to show them reasonably quickly where you're taking them.
3. You have to end in a way that encourages a next step of some kind.
4. You have to chunk up your writing and how you present it so that people can scan and read.

Drawing people in requires a good title, sometimes an appealing photograph, and a leading paragraph that makes someone want to know more about what you have to say. You can do this many ways. You can start with a kind of mystery or adventure opening. You can connect with someone's heart. You can be clear on how they'll benefit from giving you their time.

Helping people see where you're going is important. A very respected colleague of mine sent me an article about public speaking that was nine pages long. I got about midway through page two and still didn't see what the point of the post was, and so it felt like 1.5 pages too many of me trying. Be clear right up front where you're taking them and what they can expect.

Ending with some kind of call to action is easy, and it also betrays the marketer in me. I've learned that we must appeal to that built-into-all-humans drive to finish something and then ask, "Okay, so now what?" We spend a lot of times in our life feeling uncertain of where to go or what to do next. In your writing, at least, you can amend this.

Some will argue with me on that last detail, but there are many reports out there showing that people just aren't reading as much as they used to. I read somewhere that the average American reads only 45 minutes a YEAR, not counting email and social media.

This means that you and I have to work extra hard to make it easier for people to read what we have to say.

Look back at the last several paragraphs and notice that they're visually "easy" to tackle. Your eye knows what to do. There are lots of subheaders. Sentences are small. The paragraphs are mostly brief. That's another reason to chunk it up.

You know why to create a writing frame. You know what goes into it. I'll give you one more sample and then it's your turn.

Reviews – A Simple Writing Frame

This would be used for writing reviews of whatever product or service you want to review.

- Title – very clear product/service name but add something to make it intriguing
- Lead them in, but don't give up the guts immediately
- Explain the product/service from your point of view, including maybe why you sought it out
- Share any important features or details
- Discuss your experience
- Give final opinion
- Show people where to buy (if favorable)

There you go. With a few tweaks, you could review restaurants, video games, movies, doctors, using this same frame. The details are what make it yours. The frame is just a way to put it all together.

Okay, your turn!

Action: Create your own writing frame using the information above as a guide. Take no more than 20 minutes to do this exercise, and if you feel brave, share with the group.

Finally, for Bigger Projects: Your Table of Contents

This is my 9th book. I've written all of them the same way. After getting an idea, I come up with a title and subtitle. I then write out a Table of Contents. I then tweak and rearrange, add and remove chapters, until I have a great skeleton for my book.

For this book, I wrote the following in an Evernote File:

Find Your Writing Voice

Introduction – Your Voice is You
Chapter 01 – Our Destination: A Great Writing Voice
Chapter 02 – The Kitchen Table Laboratory of Writing
Chapter 03 – Use A Simple Writing Frame
Chapter 04 – Make Those Words Match The Real You
Chapter 05 – How to Find Topics to Write About
Chapter 06 – Project Thinking – How to Get More Done
Chapter 07 – The World is Waiting to Hear From You

I then emailed it to Jacq (my fiance) and asked her what she thought was missing or any changes needed. None, she said (and Jacq is a very picky reader, and quite a bibliophile so I trust her advice).

And thus, I had framed the book I planned to write for you. I'm writing it one sentence at a time in the order of the chapters, going back every now and again and adjusting what I've written to match information that spans chapters.

I do that by doing a kind of "mini" Table of Contents in every chapter. All the subheadings you see in this chapter started out as just a stack of lines, and then I reviewed the flow, added and removed, and then started writing into each part under each subheader.

That's how I write books. Not how everyone does. But if you like it, it can be how you do it, too.

I mentioned that this chapter would be a bit small. That's because we've got more pressing work to attend in the coming chapters. When you get a frame you like, add it to your area where you're storing all your writing notes. You'll want to refer to it a lot until it becomes second nature to you.

—

4

CHAPTER 04 - MAKE THOSE WORDS MATCH THE REAL YOU

Chris Brogan

Chapter 04 – Make Those Words Match The Real You

Writing can be tricky. We have an idea in our head and we can't exactly express it. Sometimes, we try to say it smarter. Other times, we worry that what we are writing doesn't make sense to anyone, so we overexplain. If we aren't the expert in a given field, we might hedge our responses and answers, messing up the writing even further.

None of this helps your reader, and it doesn't help you much, either.

The work of getting your writing to match your intentions and also the best version of your spoken voice is the core of what we're working on together. We're not trying to over stylize your voice. We're not trying to make you something that you're not. But we are seeking the best version of how you speak and making that your writing voice.

What follows is my best advice on how to tease, coax and encourage a great writing voice out of you. Ultimately, you are responsible for developing your voice. I can't hand you one. But here are the tools you'll need to get that process to work for you. Plus, you can always connect with the group and practice with them for even more success.

Study What Makes Other People's Voices Great

I love certain speakers, actors, and writers because of their amazing voices and styles. I love how people can make something purely theirs. I love stylistic writing every bit as much as I appreciate raw writing.

A few of my favorite voices:

- Chuck Palahniuk – author of Fight Club and Choke and others.
- E. Annie Proulx – her book, The Shipping News, changed my life with the terse brevity of her writing style. (And yes, I had to say both

"terse" and "brevity." Until you read the book, you won't get it.)
- Charles Bukowski – raw, dirty, and quite a slice of life
- James Altucher – my friend and modern Bukowski, if Charles were a former hedge fund manager and entrepreneur
- Pema Chodron – her writing is from the heart and teaches me a modern Buddhist perspective
- JC Herz – her book, Learning to Breathe Fire, is about CrossFit (which I'm not into), but her writing style kept me turning every page.

I could do the same with actors and TV personalities, but they'd be mine. Who are some of yours? Feel free to share with the group.

When I say "study," pick up samples of the work you really admire. Find out what in the writing works for you, speaks to you. Jot notes about it. If you like a certain genre, you'll start to see themes of what people say quite often. Write down sentences or phrases that you like.

What do they have in common? What could you steal and then make your own? What are you reacting to in the first place?

From my list above, I'll give you my quick notes:

- Palahniuk – his raw descriptions that turn normal things strange

- Proulx – brevity
- Bukowski – grit and dirty TRUE writing
- Altucher – ditto Bukowski
- Chodron – proof I'm not any more broken than anyone else
- Herz – I don't know. Magic. Need more studying

Even looking at that list, I can tell you how I've stolen parts of all these styles (and more) over the years. Nothing is ever truly unique. But I can tell you that the more we practice this kind of alchemy, the more words can become our own.

I want to brag for a moment.

A Quick Self-Serving Brag

I was interviewed to be part of a documentary called The Rise of the Entrepreneur by Eric Worre. He interviewed many famous and important people, and he also interviewed me. Eric said to me on the night that the film was going to be released that my interview contained the most unique language, the most interesting turns of phrase, and that it was hard to slice down to just a few tiny bits because they liked everything I had said.

The lead camera guy said the same thing later, corroborating the compliment.

I'm bragging because I want you to know that my style comes from a lot of places, but that how I employ it was recognized by people as sounding fresh, new and unique. Where others re-quoted themselves, or spoke in well worn cliches, I was able to use my voice to stand out amongst a field of giants.

That's what you and I are working on together.

Action: Take 20 minutes to write down a list of people whose voices you admire and some material to study. For every person, write at least a sentence or two on what makes you appreciate their voice and style. And as always, please feel free to share with the group.

See Everything as Rough Wood in Need of Sanding and Stain

Remember that very few (probably less than 1%, if that) of people write something once and it's perfect. More often than not, you'll get an idea. Somewhere on the way to the page, it gets mangled. You start strong, but then it goes wonky. Or you've got an idea but it's buried about twenty sentences in.

Does this resonate at all?

With a lot of practice (that Gladwell 10,000 hours kind), you will get a lot closer to your goal on the first try. But for most people, you've got to get into the practice of putting down the first sentences and then the first paragraphs, and then work through the rough draft, and then go back and work it up.

The Five Pass Editing Process – Sanding and Staining That Wood

To do this, think about at least five passes:

> 1. Get the idea onto the page. Just blurt it out.
> Go back to Chapter 1 and the whole goal/
> destination thing but then get your draft out.
> 2. Edit one is for the obvious messes. Did you
> use some wrong words? Does it make sense?
> Does it get you from idea one to the call to
> action?
> 3. Edit two is for voice. How do you make it
> sound more like your voice? Have you used
> cliches or other people's language?
> 4. Edit three is for chopping out the fat. Have
> you over explained? Have you repeated yourself
> unnecessarily? Kill whatever doesn't make sense
> or work. As writers say, "Kill your babies."
> 5. The final edit is the "out loud" test. Read your
> piece out loud and make sure it sounds like
> something a human would say to another
> human. (This is the hardest one.)

Like I said, as you log more and more hundreds and
then thousands of hours writing, you'll see that some of
these stages get mashed together a little bit. I write such
that steps 1,2, and 3 are mostly handled in the same pass.
When I skip steps 4 and 5, however, it's to my peril. We
all benefit from editing – your reader, most of all.

That second edit in step 3 (boy, that's not confusing) is
something we'll talk about more in the next segment.

Action: Write 300 words on the topic of "If I Had Another Life." But that's just the writing. Now, run this piece through the five pass editing process we just explained. If you like what you come up with, feel free to share with the group.

What Makes You You

People get voice mixed up with a lot of things. For instance, a lot of people assume that having a "catch" phrase is part of having your own unique voice. It's not. However, some of your verbal tics are part of that voice.

It becomes really interesting once you start training yourself to hear the verbal tics of others (and eventually yourself). You'll hear them over and over. Jacq and I (both notorious people watchers and eavesdroppers) love to repeat other people's verbal tics to each other.

- The waitress at the steak house – "Not a problem."
- The arresting officer (on COPS) – "Okay? Okay? Okay?" (He said this the way you might say um.)
- Jacq's insistence on using words like "bestest" and "gazilliondy."

What's much harder are picking out your own. When I go back to read what I've written, it's hard for me to see what's a tic or something I repeat, except for a few clearing ones.

- Things – I say this all the time.

- Tricky – I use this a lot.
- But – I start a LOT of sentences with "but" and then go back and remove them. Evidently, I love the word. I love buts.

What really makes you you is a mix of your perspective, your word choice, your experiences, and how clearly you represent yourself. Let's talk about that more. Let's move it from the ideas above to something tangible.

Better Define Your Writing Voice

Who are you when you're writing? Are you the teacher, the boss, the wise friend, the curious student? Are you the voice of authority or the wise ass? Do you swear, or do you keep it clean? What about pop culture references? Are you even hip, bro?

There's so much more that goes into this. You might be the kind of person who uses lots of analogies and metaphors. You might like to ask questions a lot, maybe even rhetorical ones. Whatever it is that makes you you is what we have to amplify.

Here's how we'll start to find it.

Action: Use the voice recorder app that comes with your phone (or download one) and talk as if you're just talking to a friend you love very much about something that interests you. Make the topic "If I ran things," and then apply it in whatever way you want to your world. Talk for about five minutes.

Then, play it back. Listen to yourself. Anything come out? What do you hear in how you talk about your topic?

We will do this more than once.

Your Voice Involves Confidence

Think about how you talk when you're in a small group of friends, and you're sharing about something you know a lot about. That's your most confident voice (one would presume). That same confidence is important in how you convey your voice when writing.

Check your writing for this. Your sentences should say "I might not know everything but I'm feeling good about what I've said here." Signs of lack of confidence include:

- Too much explaining
- Too much sharing of your qualifications

You can always send some of your writing to friends that you trust and ask them, "Does this read as if I'm confident?" If they say yes or if they say no, ask what makes them say that. This will help you identify when you're writing more confidently than not.

Let's talk about how to get your voice into your work.

What Has to Go In There

Your perspective is important. Your experience matters. Even if you're writing about something from the point of view of not knowing much about it, your goal is to convey your take on what you're experiencing.

If the writing is personable, you need to make sure people see you in the writing. If it's more professional, then you have to use a more tightened up writing style where it's not full of slang or quirks or personality.

Think for a moment about what comprises your voice in the real world. What are the positives of how you communicate? Where do people find it difficult to understand you? This is what has to go into your mindset when writing.

What Gets Left Out

It's important to Leave out an overabundance of chatty language (Get it?). If you're prone to say "You know" at the beginning or end of most sentences, do not carry this over into writing. Leave out long explanations. Skip slang, unless it's definitively part of how you speak. Use smaller words, unless it's vital that you use big ones.

Cut from your writing anything that doesn't serve the main point. Take out the "extra" story material. Keep it tight.

Be Bolder (But Only A Bit)

We talked about confidence. When you write a piece, make a statement. Don't waffle. Be straightforward. Say what you intend to say and write towards that. If you say too many people are fat and they need to improve their diet an exercise, say it. Say it even more boldly, if you want.

But only if this is close to who you are. The goal, always, is to augment who you are. But be the best of you that you can bring to the page. Because, why not?

To be bold, use more definitive words. I love coffee, instead of "coffee is okay." "People are only getting fatter and we have to take action" instead of "Obesity is a challenge that faces us all."

Keep it Real

I loathe the word authentic because it's overused. To call oneself that is like calling yourself a genius or a guru (don't). It's also hard to explain what it means to be authentic. But you have to be.

The nearest I can come to explaining this to you is by saying that it's important to match what you say to who you are and what you do. There's a tendency amongst people (not just writers) to idealize how they portray themselves when writing something down. We put our virtual best food forward.

And while it's good to put forth the "polished" you, there's a huge difference between a little written "touch up" versus a full fledged "Photoshop job." Make sense?

Okay, two tests to apply to your writing and then we're out of here.

The School Recital Test

Double check that your writing never sounds like you're back in seventh grade at age 12 and standing in front of the class. "I love turtles. Turtles are a great animal. They are a reptile. Reptiles like turtles are exciting to me."

Too much repetition is a bad thing. Too many fluff sentences that don't add to the post are a bad thing. Sometimes, on the way to our point, we might repeat. Other times, we "stuff in words" because we had a certain page count in mind. Don't stuff words. People will know. It always come off sounding seventh grade school recital.

I've got another test. This one's pretty important.

The "Out Loud" Test

This is one of the most important parts of finding your voice. It's also where I somehow skip a step quite often. It's as simple as it sounds: read your work out loud before you publish. No more, no less. You'll learn a lot about your writing from what it sounds like out loud.

In our five editing steps above, I gave this its own step for a reason. It's probably one of the most important parts of finally getting the voice in your head to match up to the one on the page, because you have to actually speak your own words aloud. You'll notice where things don't make sense, where they sound "fake," and where you can probably trim up your writing to get your points across more clearly.

Practice is the Key

You'll note that I've given you plenty of writing practice throughout the book. If you've been skipping it, don't be a poop. Go back and do it. The practice is the key. There's a mountain of difference between understanding something versus doing it.

There's a quote that I can't put my finger on about how sex and jazz are alike in that it doesn't help anyone to just talk about it. That's true with writing.

When you're starting a new project, for instance, just get something out there. Put out the first draft. If it's blogging, post. Get something in play. You learn by doing, not by reading. Reading is just the first step.

Let's move forward.

—

5

CHAPTER 05 - HOW TO FIND TOPICS TO WRITE ABOUT

Chris Brogan

Chapter 05 – How to Find Topics to Write About

If you've ever heard of SEO, Search Engine Optimization, it is the art and science of helping web pages hit the top of the page on Google searches. I rank highly for a couple of things (some of them kinda weird). I rank for "Chris," believe it or not. Just type "Chris" into your Google and you'll likely find me in the top 3-4 answers worldwide.

I also rank for "Blog Topics." It was a kind of lark. I wrote out a post a long time ago on my site, chrisbrogan.com , called "100 Blog Topics I Hope You Write." It wasn't that hard to do for me. I write daily. I come up with topics daily. So I did it.

I made a course called Blog Topics a little later, then a Master Class for that, and basically built a business that started around something as simple as giving people topics to blog about. To this day, almost five years later, it's still one of the top 3 posts on my site. Every day.

Needless to say, I guess I'm qualified to tell you about how to find topics to write about. If that's something you're struggling with, I'm your guy for it. I'll give you some topics and I'll also talk you through techniques and methods to get your own topics going.

For writing of all kinds, by the way, not just blogging. While I'm "by the way-ing" you, these are nonfiction suggestions. These are just something to get your juices flowing. You can write about whatever you want to write about.

What Goes Into a Good Article or Post or Story or Newsletter

When it comes to nonfiction, people want to be informed and/or entertained. They want both, actually. Our choice of entertainment usually informs us in some way (though it's probably hard to say shows that I watch like Rick and Morty & Archer don't do a lot of informing). Even when you're talking about something important, we need the information to be entertaining.

People don't need to have strictly original topics and ideas to read about, but you have to talk about your topics in original ways. Sometimes, it's as easy as taking a new perspective. Other times, it's a matter of coming at an old topic with new eyes.

Let's get into the meat of this. Let's talk about how to gather up ideas and then I'll give you even more tools for coming up with material. I promise it'll be helpful.

How to Collect Ideas

I have a really simple way of gathering up my ideas. I have a folder on Evernote that I call IdeaMachine, after James Altucher's idea in his book, Choose Yourself. In it, I gather up ideas for books, for blog posts, for articles, etc.

I'll tell you what James taught me: write ten ideas a day. Every day. It's what I do. The reasons are twofold:

> 1. It keeps me fresh with idea creation.
> 2. It means I always have something to write about.

I collect ideas by jotting things into Evernote and sometimes on scraps of paper. I take ideas in whenever I get them, instead of waiting for some appropriate time. I keep index cards by the bed, etc. I'm ready whenever ideas get stuck in my head.

And my secret weapon? Pictures. I take photos of ideas all the time. I shoot random photos all the time. Sometimes, I don't even remember why I took the photo.

But from these images come ideas. I saw Jacq's photo of a coffee pot with steam rising from it and it made me think of a simple article about what separates good service from great (the little details). She shot some pictures of pizza and I thought about the fact that some of us like deep dish and others like thin crust.

Photos are a great way to generate ideas.

Action: Start an IdeaMachine today. Open up Evernote or use index cards or whatever. But commit to adding five ideas a day. When you get up to speed, move up to ten. If you feel like it, share with the group.

Take a Picture; It'll Last Longer

With regards to photos, unless you are visually impaired, I can tell you that using photos to keep your thoughts moving is powerful. Collect photos for ideas. Screenshot everything that excites you. Clip things out of magazines.

One great way to develop your voice is to keep feeding your brain. Some people can't help themselves. They have to consume everything as often as possible. Make that you. Read a lot. Watch a lot of movies. Keep thinking about how everything does or doesn't relate to what you want to write about. Once you see the world with that lens more often, it's amazing how much material shows up.

It's like the red car theory. You buy a red car and suddenly everyone has a red car. Use visuals to stimulate your idea collection. I promise it'll help.

Why Hasn't Anyone?

I once visited a Boston area startup and they had dry erase paint on every wall but a few. That meant that people could write with dry erase markers on most of the walls in the building. One day, someone took a marker and started to write "Why hasn't anyone.." on the not-dry-erase wall. Probably "Why hasn't anyone ever written on this wall?" Answer: um, it's not dry erase. Just regular paint.

But for me, the question was magical. Think about it. "Why hasn't anyone…" Think of all the ways you can move forward from that question. "Why hasn't anyone written about food from the perspective of someone who just likes to eat it?" "Why hasn't anyone written a book about how to paint with shotguns?" And so on.

If you want to start filling up your Ideas file, answer that question.

Jump Over the Fence

We see things from our perspective. Heck, a huge part of this book is about how important that is. But sometimes, most everything that is written about a subject comes from one side of the fence instead of the other.

For instance, what if a flight attendant wrote about travel instead of the typical travel stories? Or how about a book from the perspective of the dishwashers at restaurants? What about the concept of health care as told from the perspective of the patient?

There are many ways to turn what you know around a little bit, or to put your own spin on the experience of something. I have a friend who is wheelchair bound and she sees cities very differently than me.

There's an old story about two land owners with an old stone wall between their properties. One day, a section of the wall fell over. One of the two land owners climbed over onto the other's side of the wall to make the repairs alongside him. It's supposed to symbolize the caring that goes into seeing something from the other person's perspective and I think it's a great way to fill up even more ideas into your notes.

This is Like That

Another really useful way to get ideas on what to write about is to think about the relationship of things, as well as analogies. Going back into the workforce after a few years away is like being back in middle school, your parents have moved, and you're at a new school where you don't know anyone and don't really know what's cool or not any more.

Find analogies and similarities and metaphors every-where. They strengthen your thinking. Google the term "cognitive resonance" and you'll see what I mean. Brains that can pick up on patterns are smarter for their work.

Now, if you want to get really nutty, you can force certain connections. "A Dog is Like a Shop Keeper." How? Beats me. I just put those two together. But imagine what will come of the exercise when you stretch your mind a bit.

Action: Write 300 words on the topic of "My Appetite is Like" where you compare your appetite (for anything, not just food) to something else. If you're feeling bold, share with the group.

Just the FAQ

When working on developing writing topics, a really simple place to start is searching around for any fre-quently asked questions (FAQ) a topic might have.

The idea is to take questions people ask about the topic you're planning to write about and incorporate them into your book/newsletter/blog post. So go to one of these places below, find questions people are asking, and mix them into your work.

For instance, if you write about shopping, maybe you'll start searching around coupon sites or luxury brand sites, etc. Looking in forums. That kind of thing. Maybe your searching will pull up a frequently asked question, like, "How do I know when the end of a selling season is?"

(Beats me. I know nothing about fashion.) That becomes your article or whatever.

Not sure where to even look for where people are talking about what you're into?

Here are a few places to peek:

- Amazon.com – people go to Amazon to review products, and there are also little micro communities hidden underneath all the various reviews.
- Reddit.com – there are subreddits (little communities) for many things. I'm always amazed at what people have put together there.
- Google Groups – http://groups.google.com has quite a few very active communities. Search there for the people you want to know and see what they're talking about.
- Yahoo Groups – http://yahoogroups.com – same thing as Google Groups
- Quora.com – this site is built strictly for asking and answering questions. Pure gold.
- And don't forget to just search. There are lots of groups and communities out there asking questions every day. Their questions can become your writing material.

This is a great source for finding what to write about and it can serve you endlessly. Almost 100% of my newsletter ideas come from answering people's questions that they've sent me or that I've seen repeated in forums where I participate.

Sequels, Prequels, Remakes, and Mashups

Have you noticed that Hollywood is obsessed with releasing and then re-releasing and reimagining everything? Toby Maguire is Spider-Man. No wait, Andrew Garfield. No, now it'll be Tom Holland. And everyone has their own vision and version.

You can do the same. You can get ideas from taking someone else's idea and recreating it as your own. I absolutely do not mean steal or copy. I mean to reimagine the idea in your own words and with your own take and perspective. Some of the most famous and successful books in the world were actually just collections of other people's ideas remastered with a stronger "hook" in place to help people understand them.

Dr. Stephen R. Covey Seven Habits of Highly Effective People is one such book, and it's one of my top five books of all time. Covey took liberally (and cited his sources) from all over the place. His work involved taking a lot of great ideas and organizing them into a very useful pattern. You can definitely do the same.

But also think of those other types of movie-like ways to write. You can take some piece of writing that you admire and think up the "prequel" (what comes before this) or the "sequel" (what comes after). You might remake it (like I mentioned before), or you might look at mashing it up.

A mashup is when you take two or more separate materials and blend them together to match a theme. There are great musical mashups and plenty of visual versions of this idea. You can definitely do the same with your writing. What if you wrote a customer service sales piece in the language of a crime thriller? What if you wrote a love letter to your sales client (but be careful here, because you know, it could come off as creepy)? What if you made a technical document into a comedy?

See how the ideas can flow?

Action: Take any one of the ways to find ideas above and use it to create a 300 word piece of your own choosing. Whatever you come up with is fine. When you're done, share with the group.

And so here we are. Another chapter down. Let's keep moving quickly. You've got to get to work writing. Don't let me hold you up.

6

CHAPTER 06 - PROJECT THINKING - HOW TO GET MORE DONE

Chris Brogan

Chapter 06 – Project Thinking – How to Get More Done

Don't skip this chapter!

I don't talk much about this, but I did time. Time as a project manager, that is. But you know, it kinda felt like prison, so you can think of it either way. I'm grateful, however, for some of what I learned from project management, both formally and otherwise, though. So I thought I'd teach you a little bit about project thinking, so that you might apply it to your writing efforts.

The Absolute Basics of Project Management

I had a teacher at a junior college (one of seven universities I attended) named Ken Hadge. If only that poor guy knew how much I wrote about him. He wore a suit that was probably very fashionable in 1978, had sprayed-in-place hair, and brought a briefcase to every class. He would put his feet up on the desk and spout wisdom and I can swear to this: his ideas on business have always been better than the "official" versions of anything I ever learned.

When he taught me about project management, he said one simple phrase: "Plenty of delicious Canadian Club." Now, while this sounded like a great idea, I suspected that there was more to it than that. Of course, it was an acronym.

P- Plan
O- Organize
D – Direction
C – Coordinate
C – Control

Plenty Of Delicious Canadian Club

Plan your project. Organize the people and materials. Provide direction for those involved. Coordinate the resources in any project. Control the outcome of the project.

Now, because you're writing, this means just you. But we can adapt this rather easily for what you have to do.

The basics of project management are this:

- Have a simple plan or destination. (We discussed this in chapter one).
- Decide how to get there (your approach).
- Align your actions such that you move towards your plan using your approach.
- Make every project have several finite, bite-sized pieces.

It might feel like a lot to think about your writing in terms of projects, but I promise, it's quite the opposite. When you have a really simple project plan in place, like the way we have a frame for your writing in place, everything aligns easier, feels like you've got someone holding your hand, and gives you confidence to work on what you want to work on, and not worry about the form and function. That's why we do it.

Why Writing is a Project

When we think of writing as a project, it allows us to break the world into better bite-sized chunks. You can think faster, work faster, and feel confident that you know where everything is with regards to your writing.

It's not fancy. You just think in terms of "I'll package this writing up" and you'll feel better about everything.

Writing is a project because you can start and stop it, work on more than one project, and you can look at yourself as something beyond just the "endless author." You're someone completing projects. It's something of power for you.

Applying Your Voice to Projects

If you think about it, all the work you've put into finding your voice can be applied to your writing almost like adding a filter to a photo on Instagram or shaking some paprika into a sauce. Only, voice is an essential building block to your writing. It's not an afterthought. But it is a decision and you can decide how your voice best applies to any of your projects.

Think of it that way. Look at every project as a chance to apply your voice in the best way to the subject at hand. Ask yourself, "What will I do to make this piece thrive because of my voice?"

Practice is a Project

Writing practice is a project. If you're not scheduling it, if you're not looking to come up with five to ten new ideas a day, you're missing out on a project that you can track and grow your success from.

But this all feels too theoretical. Let's move into the practical, shall we?

The Three Project Types for This Book (And Your Project)

There are three basic projects types for you to start with on your writing projects. You can steal these plans, use them, and adapt them to your interests. Consider these your templates.

- **Writing Practice**

  - What is the goal of this practice?
  - How much time can I allot? (20 minutes?)
  - How many words, roughly?
  - What do I need before I begin?
  - How will I evaluate what I produce?
  - Go! (Write!)

- **Writing for Your Project**

  - What is the goal of this piece?
  - How much time can I allot?
  - How many words?
  - What do I need to get across?
  - What do I need my reader to feel/do?
  - How will I evaluate what I produce?
  - Go!

- **Idea Collection**

- Do I have a place for my ideas? (Evernote/Index Cards)
- What do I need to gather?
- Are they for a specific project?
- How much time should I allot for this at any given time?
- How many new ideas will I bring in every day?
- Go! (Gather those ideas!)

Those are three simple project plans. You can edit them to match your reality, but don't stop there. Think about what you need to incorporate from previous lessons and stick that in. Think about what your projects are and work up project plans for those.

- Book writing plan (chapter by chapter, if you want)
- Email writing plan (use a frame)
- Blog post plan

Simply put together the steps of any project, without much fuss, and then follow from that plan. It will definitely improve all the work you've set yourself up to accomplish.

This is officially the shortest chapter in the book. No reason. I just didn't want to freak you out by making this chapter seem long, difficult, or boring.

Hey! One more chapter and then you're free to go make amazing things happen. Well, more amazing things. ?

7

CHAPTER 07 - THE WORLD IS WAITING TO HEAR FROM YOU

Chris Brogan

Chapter 07 – The World is Waiting to Hear From You

This is it, young Padawan! We're ready to head out and do all kinds of writing. The goal of this chapter is to give you a pep talk, review what you already know, and give you another pep talk. Did I mention there will be pep talks?

Confidence is The Core of Your Voice

If I wrote "hey you, be confident," and just finished the book there, it'd be true. But it would also be a really short book, and you wouldn't give me any money for it. That said, it is true: confidence in who you are, what you represent, and what you have to share are what matters most.

Confidence is not arrogance. Know that. Confidence just means that you feel sure of what you are saying. It doesn't mean that you can't sometimes be wrong. It doesn't mean that everyone else is a jerk and you are amazing. It just means that you feel like what you are saying is important and helpful.

You build confidence with practice. You improve confidence with putting more simple wins on the board for yourself. You develop even more confidence when you start to see and feel for yourself that your writing is improving.

One quick note: neither praise nor criticism are helpful to you. This is my bias as a Buddhist, but it's true. Hoping that your writing pleases someone else is fairly human, but hanging your own self worth on whether someone says they like or don't like your writing is a bad plan. When you write to please someone other than yourself, you set yourself up for failure. You be the judge of you. It's okay to look for advice, and get feedback, but even then, stay in control of your opinions. Be the judge for yourself.

People Need to Know What You Have to Say

One protest that writers have is that "someone else has already written this before." But they haven't heard it from you and in your way. That's important to note.

"But I'm not an expert," you'll protest. Perfect. The World has too many experts. Instead, be someone with an opinion. Someone who can be helpful. Someone who is out here writing so that you can give others something entertaining and informative.

"People don't 'get it!'" Your idea, that is. Who cares if some people don't get it? (By the way, that's who didn't get it. Someone. Usually one person.) Someone else will. And they'll love it.

My favorite book that I ever wrote was The Freaks Shall Inherit the Earth. It's actually kind of an owner's manual for entrepreneurs. I wrote it for my kids, who are too weird to get "normal" jobs. I don't really care if no one else gets it. And plenty of people didn't. It wasn't very successful, officially. But it's still my favorite, and it's pretty good.

And guess what? I get emails from people from China all the time about that book. I have no idea why China over anywhere else. But really nice letters. Personal ones. Very much asking me for help or ideas about their lives. So it's worth it.

People need to know what you have to say. I promise.

It's Been Done Before, But Not By You

Everything has been done. Most rock songs use the same exact three or four chords. Most country songs can be laid on top of each other and will line up closely. And yet, people like rock and country music.

You have a new take on what you're writing about, and people need to see it. It might not be earth shattering. Nothing I write is earth shattering. All I aim for is helpful and entertaining. That's it.

You should do the same.

Embrace the Weird

I saw a video of two people I know acting a bit goofy. They were doing this as part of a project. One of the people really sold it. He was completely into the moment. And as dopey as he looked, it also felt very real and very "right," if that makes any sense.

The other person knew that he looked foolish. He was worried that he looked foolish. And it messed up the whole experience. It would be like half diving into a pool. It's messy and it ultimately hurts.

Be you and be you 100%. If you're weird, be weird. If you curse like a sailor, then hey, go for it. If you get crazy ideas, share them.

Not everyone will love what you do. But someone will.

Someone always does. And if you get enough of those someones, you're in business.

The Best You is What People Deserve

Learn to write in your voice. Learn to edit your work using the five pass process we built together. Deliver your ideas in their bold wonderfulness. And know that this is what people want from you. They want the best of you.

Not that "Oh *.deity, I have to be amazing" kind of best. I mean the best version of you. Put your work out there. Don't second guess your work to death. Get it out there.

Deliver a big kapow experience. People will appreciate it so much more. No reason to go small, go half, or hide who you are. Be bold. We need you!

Start on Small Projects and Build Wins

The best way to get started is to start small. Maybe launch a secret hidden blog on http://WordPress.com . Make it something where you just lob out some writing, hit publish, and don't tie yourself too intensely to it.

Or start a newsletter using something like Tinyletter. Invite a few friends to join to start. And as you move forward, practice everything you've picked up in this book.

A lot of small wins build confidence. Remember that. Publish before you're ready. Try small projects before big ones. Get more and more work out there so that you feel more and more confident.

Will you fail? Man, I sure hope so. If you don't fail, you're not trying hard enough. You've got to fail. There are many lessons you can only learn through failure. Make lots of mistakes. Learn a ton. And thrive.

If Ever You Write a Book

If you've been practicing and writing, you might have it in your head to write a book. That's beautiful. And also madness. It's both.

When I tell people I've written nine books, they say "wow!" as if it's an accomplishment. I tell them almost immediately, "No, it's more like an addiction." A beautiful one, and one that can help more people than it hurts, most times, I guess, but I think of it more as a curse than a wonderful gift.

That said, if writing a book is your deal, then use this whole book to get you there. Yes, it's mostly about voice. But there are also a lot of tips and ideas in here that will help you write a full fledged nonfiction book. (Don't trust me for fiction. Get Story Grid by Shawn Coyne.)

You'll need practice. You'll need project management. You'll want to chunk things down. You'll need a frame (a Table of Contents in this case). And you'll need confidence and discipline and a perspective and a goal/destination and all that.

Start with your goal. Write your Table of Contents. Ask yourself whether it makes sense and whether people will understand. Draft out the chapters a bit, using subheadings as your way points. And then show just that to a very trusted friend and ask if what you have there (basically a skeleton) makes sense. If even vaguely yes, start writing.

I believe in you. You can really nail this. Go for it!

Get In Touch

Okay, we've come to the end of the road. That's it. The book is done. Finished. You've gotta get out of here and start writing your own damned stuff. Seriously, scram.

But if you want to get in touch with me, just email chris@chrisbrogan.com . It's me. Yes, I answer my own mail, weirdo. Who else would do it?

I'm always happy to connect.

Okay, that's it. No more sentimental goodbyes. Go write stuff. That's what matters to me. That you get something out of this book and take action. Good? Good!

(And thank you!)

About the Author

Chris Brogan is the New York Times bestselling author of 9 books including this hot little baby. He is CEO of Owner Media Group delivering skills to the modern entrepreneur. If you want to win more in life and business, check him out.
Chris lives in Massachusetts and is engaged to Jacqueline Carly (who is the inspiration for this book because she said she

needed this). Between them, they have three wonderful and creative kids.

When he's not writing books, Chris plays video games (XBOX1) and is into nerdy stuff like superhero movies, comics, and all that jazz. He lifts weights sometimes, but not as often as Jacq.

Printed by Amazon Italia Logistica S.r.l.
Torrazza Piemonte (TO), Italy

55550077R00051